WE THE PEOPLE

Great Women of the American Revolution

by Michael Burgan

Content Adviser: Julie Richter, Ph.D.,
Independent Scholar and Consultant,
Colonial Williamsburg Foundation

Reading Adviser: Rosemary G. Palmer, Ph.D.,
Department of Literacy, College of Education,
Boise State University

COMPASS POINT BOOKS
MINNEAPOLIS, MINNESOTA

Compass Point Books
3109 West 50th Street, #115
Minneapolis, MN 55410

Visit Compass Point Books on the Internet at *www.compasspointbooks.com*
or e-mail your request to *custserv@compasspointbooks.com*

On the cover: Mary Hays McCauley (Molly Pitcher) at the Battle of Monmouth

Creative Director: Terri Foley
Managing Editor: Catherine Neitge
Art Director: Keith Griffin
Photo Researcher: Marcie C. Spence
Designer/Page production: Bradfordesign, Inc./Les Tranby
Cartographer: XNR Productions, Inc.
Educational Consultant: Diane Smolinski

Library of Congress Cataloging-in-Publication Data
Burgan, Michael.
    Great women of the American Revolution / by Michael Burgan.
       p. cm.—(We the people)
    Includes bibliographical references and index.
    ISBN 0-7565-0838-X
1. United States—History—Revolution, 1775-1783—Women—Juvenile literature. 2. Women—United States—History—18th century—Juvenile literature. 3. Women—United States—Biography—Juvenile literature. I. Title. II. We the people (Series) (Compass Point Books)
    E276.B87 2004
    973.3'082—dc22   2004016325

TABLE OF CONTENTS

Women During Wartime 4

Few Rights, Many Duties 8

The Home Front 15

Close to Battle 20

Soldiers and Spies 24

Daring Messengers 31

War of Words 34

Political Power 38

Glossary 42

Did You Know? 43

Important Dates 44

Important People 45

Want to Know More? 46

Index 48

WOMEN DURING WARTIME

Historians have long studied the men who sought independence and fought the battles of the American Revolution. For many years, however, they ignored the women who contributed to the efforts during this difficult time. Even though most women did not have the opportunity to take public roles in government or fight on the battlefields, they still had an impact on the historic events of this period.

In 1775, after more than 10 years of arguments and conflict between Great Britain and its American colonies, war finally broke out. British troops and Massachusetts militia fought the first battles of the American Revolutionary War at Lexington and Concord in April 1775. The following year, as the war raged on, the colonies declared their independence in July 1776. The Americans' ultimate victory, more than six years later, secured this independence.

4

The first battle of the Revolutionary War took place on Lexington Green on April 19, 1775.

During the American Revolution, the people who supported independence from Great Britain were called patriots. Their leaders were men. So were the generals and almost all of the troops fighting on the battlefield. Off the battlefield, patriot women ran family farms and businesses.

Patriot women defend their home as a Minuteman leaves for battle.

They helped the soldiers in the field. A few worked as spies or picked up guns to fight the British. Some women spoke out publicly in the battle for independence. These women included writers and Native Americans who held important positions in their tribes.

Not all women sided with the patriots. The Americans—men and women—who sided with the British during the war were called loyalists. The women of loyalist families tried to help the British. Some of these women also served as spies. Other loyalists left the colonies for England or Canada because they feared the patriots would harm them.

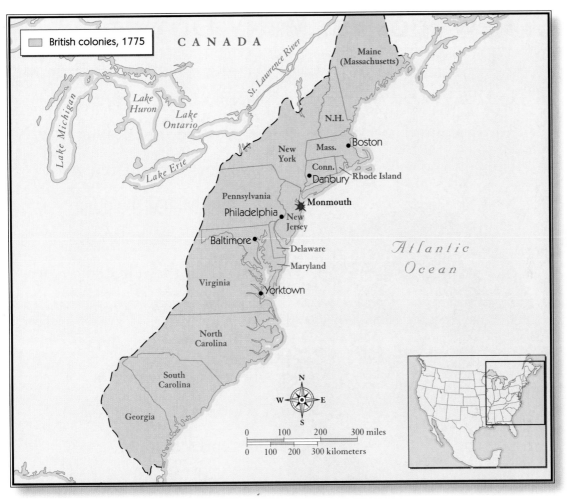

The Revolutionary War was fought throughout the colonies.

Whichever side they were on, the women who defended their causes put themselves and their families at great risk. Yet they could not remain silent or uninvolved, which took great courage.

FEW RIGHTS, MANY DUTIES

In 1776, Abigail Adams wrote to her husband, John, a patriot leader from Massachusetts. Abigail was concerned about how women would be treated during and after the war. She told her husband that he and the other leaders should "remember the ladies" when they created a new government. She wrote, "We will not hold ourselves bound by any laws in which we have no voice or representation."

Women in colonial America had few legal rights. They could not vote or run for political office. Most young girls received little formal schooling, unless their parents were wealthy

Abigail Adams

8

Colonial women were expected to take care of the household and raise the children.

and hired tutors for them. Fathers had complete control over their single daughters, and parents expected their daughters to marry and raise children. Many religious groups at that time believed women were made to have children. Married women were considered their husband's property to do with as he wished.

Female indentured servants and African-American slaves had even fewer rights. They could not marry without their masters' permission. In fact, slave marriages were not considered legal. They also faced beatings from violent masters who knew the courts usually ignored their cruelty. Courts assumed that masters would not harm their servants or slaves to the point that they could not work. Servants, slaves, and even wives sometimes ran away to escape such brutal treatment.

In most homes, married women had many chores. Taking care of their families and running their households kept women busy every day of the week. Women kept cooking fires burning and made their families' meals. Many meals featured vegetables and herbs that the women grew in small gardens outside their kitchen. Mothers made their families' clothes, then washed them when they were dirty and fixed them if they ripped. Women also made such things

Cooking was one of the many chores performed by colonial women.

as soap, candles, butter, and cheese. They performed
these chores while raising their children, teaching their
daughters how to manage a household, and sometimes
helping their husbands with farmwork.

11

In addition to their other duties, some women helped their husbands on the farm.

Despite their hard lives, some women made money through farming or business. A woman could sometimes receive property after the death of a husband or of a father, if she was unmarried or widowed. Otherwise, her inheritance became part of her husband's property. Some women ran family farms while their husbands or fathers were away. During the 1740s, Eliza Lucas of South Carolina ran three plantations for her father.

She helped introduce a new crop to the colony—indigo. The plant was used to make a blue dye, and indigo soon became a very important export for South Carolina. Eliza Lucas, who married Charles Pinckney, was a devoted patriot. Her two sons served during the American Revolution, and later she was friendly with George Washington.

Some widows ran businesses that once belonged to their husbands, while others opened up their own. Women performed a variety of services, including making clothes, operating taverns, and taking in boarders. Some women even did work usually done by men, such as making guns or shoeing horses.

One Boston woman reported that she could make "tea-kettles and coffee pots, copper drinking pots, brass and copper sauce pans ... and fish kettles."

Women did not have equal rights, but they worked equally hard—if not harder—than men. Their hard work became even more important as the American colonies prepared for war.

14

Churning butter was a hard task usually done by women.

THE HOME FRONT

In 1765, the British government planned to place a tax on documents and papers used in the colonies. The law was called the Stamp Act. Many Americans protested the Stamp Act. Patriots in many cities formed groups called the Sons of Liberty. They led the efforts to end the tax and protect the rights of American colonists.

Patriots burn documents in New York City to protest the hated Stamp Act in 1765.

15

In some cities, women formed the Daughters of Liberty. They helped the patriots boycott British goods. They used spinning wheels to make their own cloth, called homespun, so Americans could stop buying clothes from Great Britain. The Daughters of Liberty also boycotted tea. They bought coffee or made herbal drinks to protest a British tax on tea.

Patriot women had even more to do after April 1775. To fight the British, the Americans created the Continental Army. States also raised militias. Young men left their farms and businesses and became soldiers. As they had in the past, women stepped in to do jobs their husbands, fathers, and sons had once done.

A colonial woman spins her own cloth so she would not have to purchase clothes from the British.

Women in Philadelphia made clothes for Continental Army soldiers.

Now the women were not only supporting their families, but also providing supplies for the troops fighting for American independence. The women raised food and made clothes for the war effort. They also faced the danger of enemy attacks. Abigail Adams worried for her safety when British ships sailed near Boston. She described how the whole city was "in confusion, packing up and carting out of town, household furniture, military stores, goods, etc." An attack never came, however, as the ships sailed away.

17

Slave women also took on extra duties as men went off to war. Some female slaves in Virginia were forced to work in industries such as iron making and shipbuilding. If food was scarce, the slaves received less than their masters and masters' families did. Some slave women ran away from their masters during the war. Slaves of patriots sought help from the British, while slaves on loyalist farms joined the patriots. Women from wealthy patriot families helped raise money and supplies for the troops. Two of the most famous female patriots were Esther Reed and Sarah Franklin Bache of Philadelphia. Esther Reed's

18

Esther Reed

husband, Joseph, was a prominent patriot, and Sarah Bache was the daughter of Benjamin Franklin, the great scientist and political leader. In 1780, Esther formed a group called the Association. The group collected money to help the American troops. Esther died of a fever soon after

Sarah Franklin Bache

forming the Association, and Bache emerged as one of its new leaders. Bache organized women to sew shirts for the Continental Army. She also ran her father's house while he was away as a diplomat representing the United States in Europe. Franklin's role made his daughter an important woman in Philadelphia.

19

CLOSE TO BATTLE

Not all women stayed at home when their male relatives went off to war. Many women and their children often followed the soldiers to the battlefield. Either they could not survive on their own at home or they simply wanted to be close to their loved ones. These women, called camp followers, cooked, washed and sewed clothes, hauled water and firewood, and nursed the sick and wounded. As many as 20,000 women helped the

Men and women faced the British army on the battlefield.

Continental Army this way. The British also relied on camp followers to perform many duties.

One woman who followed the Continental Army was Sarah Osborn, from New York. She went with her husband, Aaron, when he joined the Continental Army. Sarah washed clothes and cooked meals for the troops under General George Washington. In 1781, she worked at Yorktown, the site of the last major battle of the Revolutionary War. She kept serving food while British guns fired all around her. She later told Washington, "It would not do for men to fight and starve too."

British General Cornwallis surrendered after the Battle of Yorktown to end the fighting.

21

Washington did not like the idea of women traveling with the troops. He feared that a wife might try to convince her husband to desert. He also feared women would slow down troop movements and have to share in the already limited supplies of food. Yet the general knew the women helped feed, clothe, and nurse his men.

Washington actually enjoyed the company of his own wife, Martha, during the war. The British and Americans usually stopped fighting during the winter,

Martha Washington (right) visited her husband and his troops during the war.

and officers' wives often traveled to their husband's winter camps. Every year from 1775 to 1781, Martha Washington left Mount Vernon, her comfortable Virginia plantation, to stay with her husband. These trips were often difficult. In 1775, the British spread a rumor that Mrs. Washington opposed the war. As she traveled, a few patriots who believed the rumor insulted her.

Mrs. Washington also disliked being close to the battlefield. At the American camp outside Boston, Massachusetts, she wrote, "I confess I shudder every time I hear the sound of a gun." Over the next few years, however, Martha proved she was dedicated to American independence. She and other officers' wives sewed clothes for the soldiers and tried to cheer up the sick or wounded.

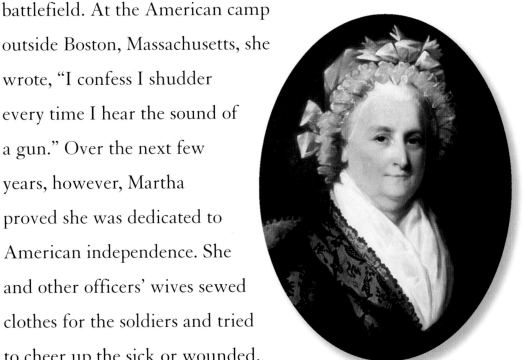

Martha Washington

SOLDIERS AND SPIES

A few brave women played roles on the battlefield. One of them was Mary Hays McCauley. She was the wife of a soldier from Pennsylvania. She followed her husband,

Mary Hays McCauley fires her husband's cannon at the Battle of Monmouth.

24

William Hays, into war and brought pitchers of water to the men firing the cannons. She and other women who performed that duty were sometimes called Molly Pitcher.

In 1778, Mary became the most famous "Molly" of all when she helped fight at the Battle of Monmouth in New Jersey. Her husband was wounded, so Mary took his place at the cannon. Another soldier described how she kept firing even when "a cannon shot from the enemy passed directly between her legs."

Another "Molly Pitcher" who followed her husband to war and stepped in for him when he fell was Margaret Cochran Corbin of Pennsylvania. She was badly injured while she fought in New York and lost the use of her left arm. In 1779, Congress gave her a military pension. Corbin was the first American woman to win that honor.

One woman did not follow a male relative into the army—she decided to enlist on her own, by pretending to be a man. In 1782, Robert Shurtleff of Massachusetts joined the Continental Army. Shurtleff was actually Deborah Sampson, a former servant and teacher. She cut her hair and hid the shape of her body to look more like a man. Since many teenage boys fought for the Americans, no one thought it strange that "Robert" did not shave. Sampson served well and was wounded in battle. A doctor finally discovered that Sampson was a woman when she went to the hospital with a fever. She was honorably discharged from the Continental Army in 1783. Sampson later went on a lecture tour to tell her story.

Deborah Sampson

Women helped generals on both sides by working as spies. An important patriot spy was Lydia Darragh of Philadelphia, Pennsylvania. During most of the war, Philadelphia served as the new nation's capital. British forces seized the city in October 1777. Darragh sometimes overheard British officers discussing their plans. She wrote down the information on tiny pieces of paper and hid them inside cloth-covered buttons on her son's jacket. Her son wore the jacket as he traveled out of the city to General Washington's nearby camp. He then gave the messages to his brother, who was a soldier there.

Once Mrs. Darragh herself delivered a message. British commander William Howe had used a room in her

A British officer questions patriot spy Lydia Darragh.

27

Lydia Darragh warned the Americans of a planned British attack in December 1777.

house to discuss plans for a sneak attack on the Americans. Darragh disobeyed a British order to stay in her room during the meeting. Instead, she silently crept up to the doorway and listened through the keyhole. The next day, she told British guards she had to go to the local flour mill. She went to the mill, but she also visited the American camp and warned about the British attack. Continental troops were ready when the British arrived, and their lives were saved.

The British also used American women as spies. The most successful of these loyalist spies was Ann Bates, a Pennsylvania schoolteacher. She acted as a peddler so she could enter the American camp. While selling such things as thread, knives, and combs, she listened for military plans. As Bates later wrote, she also "had the opportunity of going through their whole army … [noting] the strength & situation of each brigade, & and the number of cannon." Bates was never caught. Shortly before the end of the war, she and her husband sailed for England. She is known as one of the greatest female spies of all time.

A letter written by Ann Bates about a fellow spy.

Peggy Shippen Arnold and child

Another loyalist woman played a large role in weakening the patriot cause. Peggy Shippen of Philadelphia married American general Benedict Arnold in 1779. Arnold had fought bravely for the patriots at many battles, but he felt Congress did not reward him for his actions. Arnold listened closely when his new wife told him he should consider working for the British. Shippen introduced her husband to Major John André, the British officer in charge of spying. He and Shippen had become friendly while the British were in Philadelphia. Arnold agreed to work with André and fight against the Americans. He is known today as the most infamous traitor in U.S. history.

DARING MESSENGERS

On the night of April 18, 1775, patriots Paul Revere and William Dawes rode through the Massachusetts countryside. They carried a warning that the British were coming. All Americans now learn about this famous "midnight ride," but few know that several women also made daring journeys to warn of British attacks.

Paul Revere warned the Americans that the British were coming during his famous ride of April 18, 1775.

A statue of Sybil Ludington stands near the shore of Lake Gleneida in Carmel, New York.

Sixteen-year-old Sybil Ludington made her own midnight ride in 1777. Her father was a colonel in the New York militia. He received news that the British were attacking nearby Danbury, Connecticut.

Colonel Ludington quickly alerted the local soldiers so they could help defend the town. Sybil took a family horse and rode 40 miles (64 kilometers) that night. At each house, she rapped on the front door with a wooden stick to wake up the troops. The patriots could not save Danbury, but Ludington had shown her bravery.

In the colony of South Carolina, Dicey Langston also carried news about an attack. Many of the neighbors around her family's South Carolina plantation were loyalists. Some of these people formed their own militia and raided patriot farms. Langston heard that a loyalist group called the Bloody Scouts was going to attack a farm near her brother's plantation. The teenager walked through forests and crossed streams to give her brother the news. The next day, he and his friends warned their patriot neighbors before the Scouts could attack.

Dicey Langston shielded her father from the Bloody Scouts. The men were so impressed with her bravery that they spared their lives.

WAR OF WORDS

Before and during the American Revolution, the patriots tried to convince Americans to join their cause. They used newspapers and pamphlets to attack British policies and promote independence. Most American women at the time were not well educated. Still, some joined this war of words against the British.

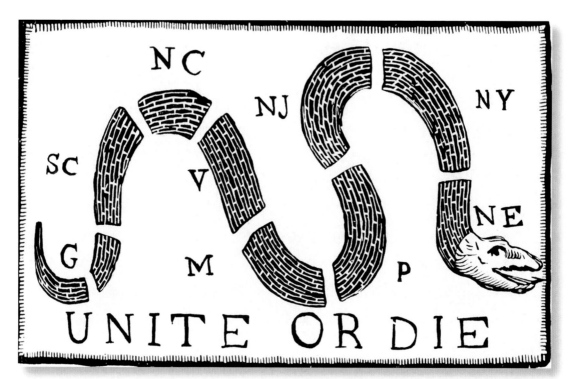

Benjamin Franklin's political cartoon urging the colonies to unite appeared in his Pennsylvania Gazette.

Mary Katherine Goddard was one of the most important printers in America. She learned how to print newspapers while working with her brother William. He published newspapers in several different cities. In 1775, Katherine took over his newspaper publishing business in Baltimore, Maryland. Two years later, Congress asked her to publish the first complete copy of the Declaration of Independence. Goddard published her newspaper throughout the war.

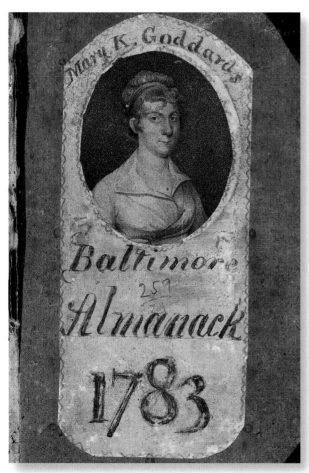

Mary Katherine Goddard published several almanacs while working in Baltimore.

Several women wrote about the war in poems, plays, and articles. Even before the war, Phillis Wheatley was a well-known African-American poet in both Great Britain and the colonies. Readers were especially

An engraving of Phillis Wheatley from her book of poems published in 1773

impressed because she was a slave. During the American Revolution, she wrote a poem honoring George Washington. In another, she wrote, "We for freedom fight." Wheatley was given her own freedom in 1773. Her last poem praised the American victory over the British. It was published in 1784, just a few days after Wheatley died.

Another talented writer was Mercy Otis Warren. She was part of an influential patriot family that included her husband, James Warren, and her older brother, James Otis. Mercy was a brilliant author who wrote plays that made fun of the British and praised American freedom. In one of her plays, a character refers to the British as "monsters" and hopes that "their glories fade, crushed in the ruins they themselves had made." Many years later, she wrote one of the first histories of the United States. The three-volume history was published in 1805 when Warren was 77 years old.

Mercy Otis Warren

POLITICAL POWER

Women clearly had some influence during the American Revolution, and their hard work helped the country win its freedom. Yet neither white nor black women could shape the political decisions made during the war. In some Native American tribes, however, women did have this power. Most tribes had male chiefs, but women could sometimes take that role. Respected women could influence what their tribes did.

The tearing down of King George III's statue in New York City symbolized the Americans' fight for freedom and new political direction.

Both the British and the Americans wanted Indian allies during the American Revolution. Many Iroquois fought for the British in New York and Pennsylvania. Their leader was Thayendanegea. The British called him Joseph Brant.

Molly Brant's picture appeared on a Canadian stamp in 1986 to commemorate the 250th anniversary of her birth.

His sister Mary (Molly) Brant was also a respected figure. She married a wealthy British official who owned land in New York. Molly Brant convinced many Iroquois to remain loyal to Great Britain during the war. The British praised her efforts. One official noted that her influence was "far superior to that of all their Chiefs put together."

39

One Native American who supported the Americans was a Cherokee woman named Nancy Ward. The Cherokee lived in the southeastern United States. Ward was called a Beloved Woman because of her bravery during a battle with an enemy tribe. As a Beloved Woman, Ward helped make political decisions and discussed treaties with other tribes. During the American Revolution, Ward supported the patriots, although most

In a painting entitled "The Confrontation," Nancy Ward (left, in pink) used her power as a Beloved Woman to save a white woman from execution by her cousin Dragging Canoe.

of the Cherokee sided with the British. Two years after the war, she helped create the first treaty between an Indian nation and the U.S. government.

During the 18th century, most American men thought women should work in the home and raise children. They never would have listened to a Mary Brant or a Nancy Ward. The men believed women were not equal to men. Even after the war, women had to fight a long time to win equal legal rights. In the war for American independence, however, women of all backgrounds proved their worth and helped create the United States.

Patriot women defended their families and their new way of life.

41

GLOSSARY

allies—countries or groups that support one another
in a conflict

boycott—a refusal to buy certain goods or do business with
someone as a form of protest

brigade—a large group of soldiers

diplomat—person who represents his or her government in
a foreign country

indentured servants—people who must work for someone for
a certain amount of time to repay travel and other expenses

militia—an army of part-time soldiers

pension—money paid regularly to people who have retired
from work or the military

plantations—large farms in the South that usually used slave
labor to grow one main cash crop such as tobacco, rice, or indigo

DID YOU KNOW?

- Mary Katherine Goddard was the first American woman to run a post office. She was named postmaster in Baltimore, Maryland, in 1775.

- Besides Deborah Sampson, at least two other women dressed as men and fought in the American Revolution. One of them was an African-American named Sally St. Claire. She died in battle. Another woman, Ann Bailey of Massachusetts, fought under the name Samuel Gay. She reached the rank of sergeant before anyone knew she was a woman.

IMPORTANT DATES

Timeline

1763	British issue the Proclamation of 1763, which prohibits settlement west of the Appalachian Mountains and angers many American colonists.
1765	American patriots protest the Stamp Act.
1775	Battles at Lexington and Concord, near Boston, Massachusetts, launch the American Revolutionary War.
1776	Congress approves the Declaration of Independence.
1777	British forces seize Philadelphia.
1781	George Washington's army defeats the British at Yorktown, the last major battle of the war.
1783	The Treaty of Paris ends the American Revolution.
1785	The U.S. government signs its first treaty with a Native American tribe, the Cherokee.

IMPORTANT PEOPLE

SARAH FRANKLIN BACHE (1743-1808)
Benjamin Franklin's daughter who helped support American troops

LYDIA DARRAGH (1729-1789)
Philadelphian who spied for the Americans when the British controlled her city

SYBIL LUDINGTON (1761-1839)
Young woman who rode through the countryside to warn the local militia about a British attack

MARY HAYS MCCAULEY (1754-1832)
Also known as Molly Pitcher, the wife of a soldier who stepped in for her wounded husband at the Battle of Monmouth and helped fire his cannon

DEBORAH SAMPSON (1760-1827)
A Massachusetts teacher who dressed as a man and fought in the war

NANCY WARD (c. 1738-1824)
Cherokee Beloved Woman who supported the patriots during the war

PHILLIS WHEATLEY (1753-1784)
African-American woman who impressed readers with her poetry and gained her freedom from slavery before the Revolutionary War

WANT TO KNOW MORE?

At the Library

Amstel, Marsha. *Sybil Ludington's Midnight Ride*. Minneapolis: Carolrhoda
  Books, 2000.

Bohannon, Lisa Frederiksen. *The American Revolution*. Minneapolis: Lerner, 2004.

Burke, Rick. *Deborah Sampson*. Chicago: Heinemann Library, 2003.

Redmond, Shirley-Raye. *Patriots in Petticoats: Heroines of the American
  Revolution*. New York: Random House, 2004.

Slavicek, Louise Chipley. *Women of the American Revolution*. San Diego:
  Lucent Books, 2003.

On the Web

For more information on this topic, use FactHound.

1. Go to *www.facthound.com*

2. Type in this book ID: 075650838X

3. Click on the *Fetch It* button.

FactHound will find the best Web sites for you.

On the Road

Colonial Williamsburg

Williamsburg, VA 23187-1776

757/220-7286 or 800-HISTORY

To see how enslaved and free

women lived during colonial times

Monmouth Battlefield State Park

347 Freehold-Englishtown Road

Manalapan, NJ 07726

732/462-9616

To tour the site of the Battle of

Monmouth and learn more about

the Revolutionary War

Look for more We the People books about this era:

The Battles of Lexington and Concord   *Monticello*

The Bill of Rights   *Mount Vernon*

The Boston Massacre   *Paul Revere's Ride*

The Boston Tea Party   *The Stamp Act of 1765*

The Declaration of Independence   *The U.S. Constitution*

The Minutemen   *Valley Forge*

A complete list of We the People titles is available on our Web site:
www.compasspointbooks.com

INDEX

Adams, Abigail, 8, 17
African Americans, 10, 36
André, John, 30
Arnold, Benedict, 30
Arnold, Peggy Shippen, 30

Bache, Sarah Franklin, 18, 19
Bates, Ann, 29
Battle of Monmouth, 25
Battle of Yorktown, 21
Bloody Scouts, 33
Boston, Massachusetts, 13, 17, 23
boycotts, 16
Brant, Joseph, 39
Brant, Mary (Molly), 39, 41
businesses, 12-13

camp followers, 20-22
Cherokee Indians, 40
chores, 10-11, 41
clothing, 10, 13, 16, 17, 19, 23
Concord, Massachusetts, 4
Continental Army, 16, 17, 19,
    20-23, 25, 26, 28
Corbin, Margaret Cochran, 25

Darragh, Lydia, 27-28,
Daughters of Liberty, 16
Dawes, William, 31
Declaration of Independence, 35

education, 8-9
equality, 8, 10, 14, 41

farming, 11, 12-13
food, 10, 17, 18, 21, 22
Franklin, Benjamin, 19

Goddard, Mary Katherine, 35

homespun cloth, 16

indentured servants, 10
indigo plant, 13
inheritances, 12
Iroquois Indians, 39

Langston, Dicey, 33
loyalists, 6, 18, 30
Lucas, Eliza, 13
Ludington, Sybil, 32

map, 7
marriage, 9, 10
McCauley, Mary Hays, 24-25
metalwork, 13
militias, 16, 32
Mount Vernon plantation, 23

Native Americans, 6, 38-41
newspapers, 34, 35

Osborn, Sarah, 21

pamphlets, 34
patriots, 5-6, 13, 15, 18, 19, 23, 32, 34
Philadelphia, Pennsylvania, 18,
    19, 27, 30
Pitcher, Molly. See McCauley,
    Mary Hays.

Reed, Esther, 18-19
Revere, Paul, 31

Sampson, Deborah, 26
shipbuilding, 18
slaves, 10, 18, 36
Sons of Liberty, 15
spies, 6, 27-30
Stamp Act, 15

taxation, 15, 16
Thayendanegea, 39
treaties, 41

Ward, Nancy, 40-41
Warren, Mercy Otis, 37
Washington, George, 13, 21, 22,
    27, 36
Washington, Martha, 22, 23
Wheatley, Phillis, 36
writers, 6, 34-37

About the Author

Michael Burgan is a freelance writer of books for children and adults. A history graduate of the University of Connecticut, he has written more than 60 fiction and nonfiction children's books for various publishers. For adult audiences, he has written news articles, essays, and plays. Michael Burgan is a recipient of an Educational Press Association of America award and belongs to the Society of Children's Book Writers and Illustrators.